W9-ATG-202

A group of angels came to the Prophet Mohammed
while he was sleeping.
Some of them said, "He is sleeping."
Others said, "His eyes are sleeping but his heart is awake."
Then one of them said, "Here is an example for this companion of yours."
And another said, "Then set forth an example for him."
One of them said, "He is sleeping."
Another said, "His eyes are sleeping but his heart is awake."
Then one of them said, "The example is that
of a man who built his house and then offered therein a banquet,
and he sent a messenger to invite the people to eat.
So whoever accepted the invitation of the messenger
entered the house and ate of the banquet.
And whoever did not accept the invitation of the messenger
did not enter the house, nor did he eat of the banquet."
Then the angels said, "Interpret this parable so he may understand it."
One of them said, "He is sleeping."
The others said, "His eyes are sleeping but his heart is awake."
And then they said,
"The house stands for Paradise
and the call-maker is Mohammed."

(Hadîth)

The month of Ramadan, the ninth month
of the Islamic calendar in which the Koran was revealed,
a guide for mankind and clear proof
of the criteria between right and wrong.
Whoever sees the crescent moon on the first night
of the month of Ramadan must observe *Saum* (fasts) that month,
and whoever is ill, or on a journey,
must make up the same number of days
on which he did not observe fasts on other days.
Allah intends ease for you.
He does not want to make things difficult for you.

(2:185)

On the nights of *As-Saum* (fasting)...
seek that which Allah has ordained for you,
and eat and drink until the white thread (light of dawn)
appears distinct from the black thread (darkness of night),
then resume your *Saum* until nightfall.

(2:187)

Allah is the Protector and Guardian of those who believe.
He brings them out from darkness into light.

(2:257)

Allah is the Light of the heavens and earth.
His light is as if there were a niche and within it a lamp.
The lamp is in a glass, like a brilliant star lit from a blessed olive tree.
The tree is neither of the east—getting its rays of the sun only in the morning,
nor of the west—getting its rays of the sun only in the afternoon,
but exposed to the sun all day long, its oil glowing forth,
though no fire has touched it.

(24:35)

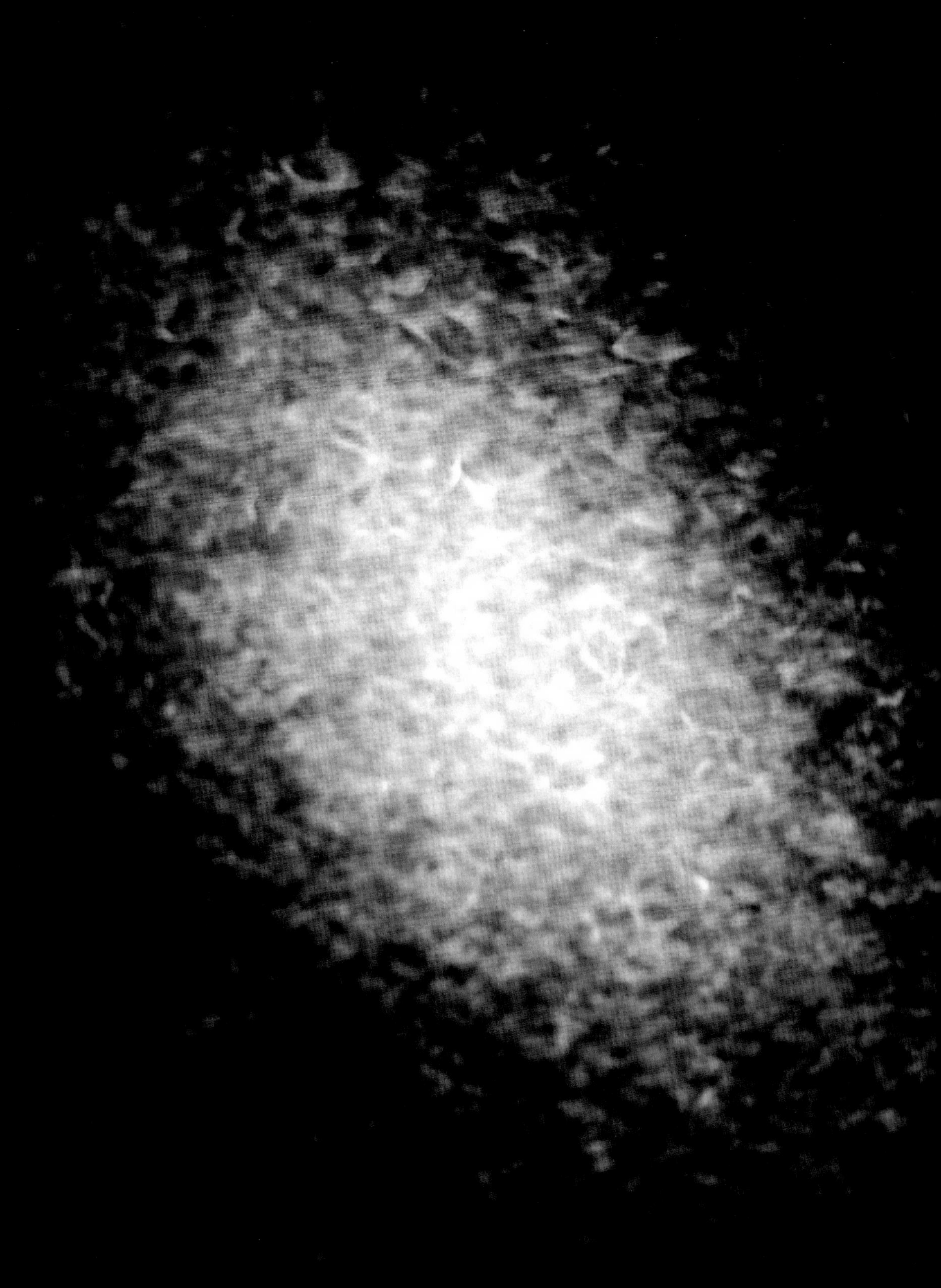

So I swear by the afterglow of sunset.
And by the night and whatever it gathers in its darkness.
And by the moon when it is full.
You shall travel from stage to stage in this life
and in the Hereafter.

(84:16–19)

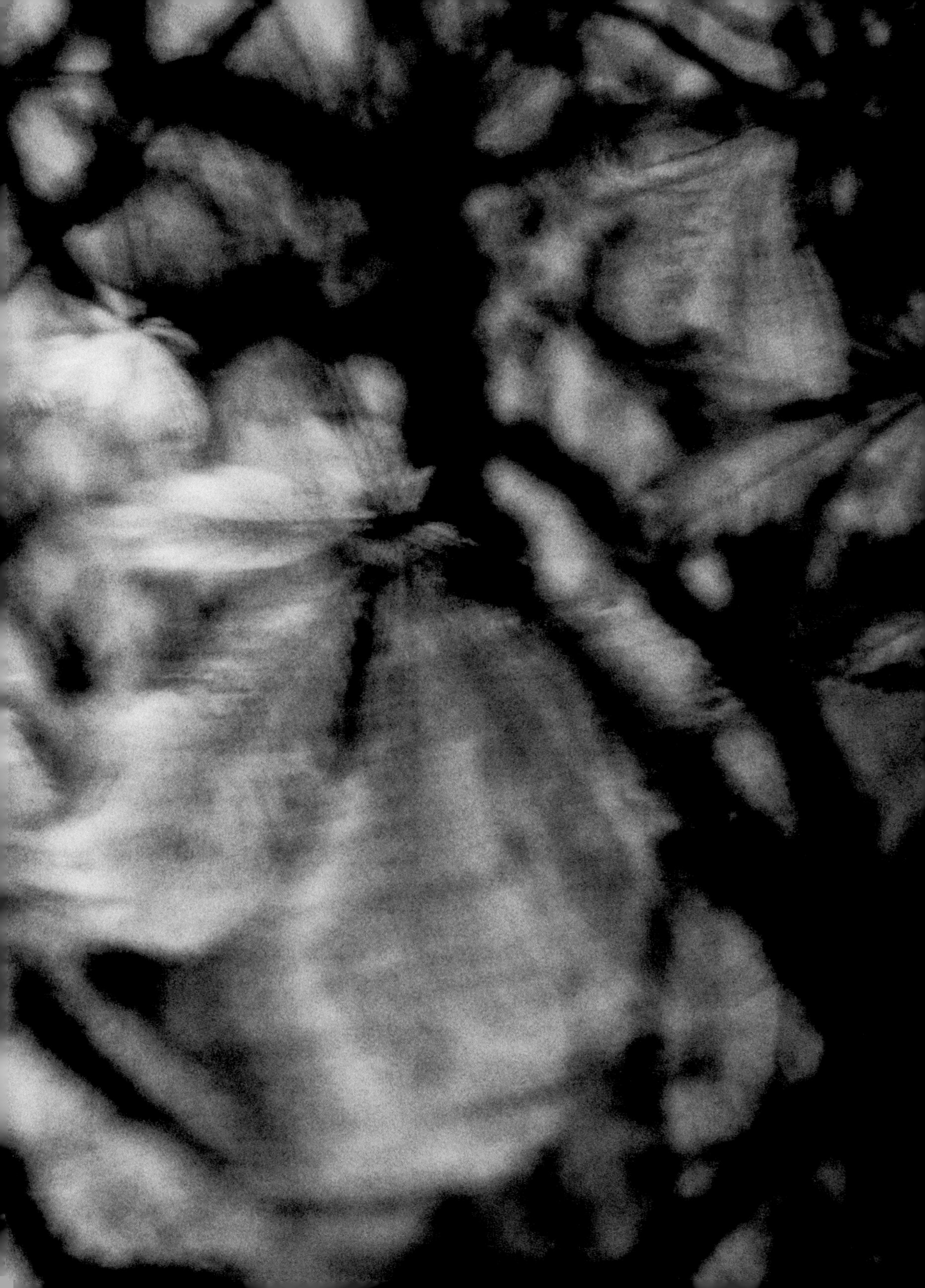

Allah has adorned the nearest heaven with lamps—
stars as decoration,
missiles to ward off the devils,
and signs to guide travelers
through the darkness of the land and sea.

(Hadîth)

A man was reciting *Sûrah Al-Kahf* (The Cave),
with his horse tethered beside him,
when a cloud descended from the sky and engulfed the man,
coming closer and closer to him.
His horse reared up as if it was afraid of something.
The next morning the man sought out the Prophet Mohammed
and told him of his experience. The Prophet said,
"That was *As-Sakînah* (tranquility or peace and reassurance, along with angels),
which descended because of the recitation of the Koran."

(Hadîth)

When the sun is wound round and its light is lost and overthrown
(the sun and the moon will be deprived of their light on the Day of Resurrection).
And when the stars fall. And when the mountains are made to pass away.
And when the pregnant she-camels are left untended.
And when the wild beasts are gathered together.
And when the seas become a blazing Fire or overflow.
And when the souls are joined with their bodies...
And when the pages of every person's deeds are laid open to be read.
And when the heavens are stripped away. And when Hellfire is set ablaze.
And when Paradise is brought near.
Then every person will know what he has brought.
So, verily, I swear by the planets that disappear by day and reappear by night,
by the planets that move swiftly to hide themselves.
And by the night as it departs. And by the dawn as it brightens.
In truth, this is the Word brought by the angel Gabriel,
a most honorable messenger, owner of power with Allah,
obeyed by the angels in the heavens,
and trustworthy.

(81)

The first group of people who enter Paradise
will shine like the moon on the night of a full moon.
The next group will glitter like the brightest star.
Their hearts will be as one,
for they will have no difference or enmity among them.

(Hadith)

RAMADAN MOON

I was born in Mogadishu in 1959. My father worked for the government of President Siad Barre as a driver. I had a good life with my parents; we had few problems. In Mogadishu, the moon and the stars were always with us. As children we would climb up into the hills around the city, while the other people crowded on to the rooftops, gazing into the sky, or boatloads of them ventured out to sea, all of us waiting for the first sight of the crescent moon which marks the start of Ramadan. That was always the happiest month of the year.

During the days of Ramadan, the women prepared food for the evening and welcomed their husbands home at night when the family would sit together to break their fast. My mother made sweetmeats, samosas, kebabs, bajia and dates—meals that smelled more delicious than at any other time of the year. It was the same in any house in the neighborhood because the parents of other children were just like our own—a real family. If someone happened to be passing a house and the people inside saw them go by, they would invite them in to share their meal. Then, when we had broken our fast, we would walk along the water's edge, taking in the evening air before following the moon to the mosque and the last prayers of the day.

When I grew older, I didn't go to school but stayed at home to help my mother in the house. Eventually my parents arranged a marriage for me, and my husband joined us in our home. It was a very happy time for me then.

But a few years later, in 1991, the fighting broke out in our country and many things changed. My parents worried because we were from a small clan with no trained militia or weapons and there was nobody to protect us. We were the victims of looting and rape, and gradually we lost everything that can be taken from a person. But at first we remained at home. We did not know where else to go and we did not want to leave our country. One woman had children who were fleeing Mogadishu for Europe and they begged her to go with them. But she asked: "In that place where you are going, will I be able to hear the Azan *(the call to prayer) in the morning?" When they told her no, she said in that case she would stay in Somalia, since she could not live without the* Azan *wakening her from sleep.*

The war brought chaos to our district. Our house was often on the front line and it was dangerous to stay anywhere for too long, so we were forced to leave our home and had to ask our relatives who lived in other parts of the city to take us in. As the fighting grew worse, I became pregnant with my first child. It was a very difficult pregnancy. When I went into labor, the fighting was so intense that we had to take refuge in the mosque—the same mosque that I had visited throughout my childhood. It was there that Fatuma, my first child, was born. There was no midwife to help me with the delivery. I had to rely on men for assistance, which for a Somali woman is very difficult. I lost consciousness during labor and afterward I was extremely weak. But we couldn't stay in the mosque for long and were forced to return to our house during a lull in the fighting.

My husband grew afraid to leave the house. He was from a minority clan and particularly at risk. So I went out to work while he stayed at home with the family. I worked as a cleaning woman and I was paid with food. But since the other Somalis were also poor, I often went for days without work, which meant that my family did not eat and I could barely produce enough milk for the baby. But time went by and the next year I gave birth to my second daughter, Aisha. I was badly undernourished and this made the pregnancy and the birth very hard to get through. This time, though, I was fortunate because I was at home, and my parents and neighbors were there to help with the delivery. The following year we were forced to flee our house again and this time we lived in the bush for four months in a small hut made from sticks and plastic sheeting. It was in the Karan district, where it was a bit safer. In that hut I gave birth to my youngest child, my son Mohammed, who is here with me.

One day in early 1999, after living with the war for almost a decade, I was at home with my children and my father when four men from one of the larger clans broke into our house carrying guns. They grabbed me and began tearing at my clothes. My father tried to protect me, shouting at them and pulling them away. Then it happened: one of the men turned and shot my father. He died immediately. Then they attacked me again. They did many violent things to me. I still have the scars where they burned me with cigarettes. I have other scars, too. Some of them have not healed. I still have medical problems because of what happened to me in this attack. My children were in the compound with me. They saw everything.

When the men had finished, they left, and my neighbor came in and took us to his house. Someone was sent to bring my mother who had been at the market and when she heard what had happened she collapsed with shock. Her blood pressure rose and we did not have enough money for a doctor. Seven days later, she died of a broken heart. We bathed her body and wrapped it in a white cloth and buried her near our neighbor's house. We could not bury her in a grave next to my father.

After that we were so afraid that the men would return, we didn't go back home but stayed in our neighbor's house. I became very depressed and afraid. But it was fortunate that my husband had been away at the time of the attack, because if he had been at home, he would have been killed. When he returned, he was very worried about me and wanted me moved to a safe place. We would be vulnerable if we stayed, because the clans often returned to places where they had already brought violence.

Before he died, my father had been afraid that he would be killed, and he had asked our neighbor, who was from a larger clan, to take care of us if anything happened to him. So our neighbor decided that the best thing for us to do would be to trade our home for a passage to a place called Denmark, where he hoped that I could be treated for my depression and other medical problems. I had never been away from Mogadishu, but I was not in a fit state to decide anything at that point, so he made all the plans for our journey. Then we discovered we did not have enough money for all of us to travel, so my husband decided that we would have to split up the family; I would take Mohammed with me, and he would take the girls with him to his family in Baidoa. It was not safe there, either, but there was nowhere else to go, and he hoped his family would protect them.

So I was separated from my husband and from Fatuma and Aisha. I cannot describe to you how hard it was for me to leave my daughters with whom I had suffered so much. And in all that time since I left them, I have had no word of whether they are safe, no news of them at all, and I have no way of knowing how to trace them.

The man who arranged our passage gave us papers and a passport, and we were put on one of the planes returning to Kenya after delivering its cargo of khat. *As soon as we landed, we were driven through the night into Tanzania, where we stayed for two days with an old woman before some men came and told me to be ready at midnight. We were then taken to the airport and put on a very large plane to take us to Denmark.*

On the way, we stopped off in Holland. At Schiphol airport I was searched and interviewed, with a Somali woman translating by telephone. My Somali identity card and the false passport I had been given were taken away and eventually we were brought to this Asylum Seekers' Center, where we have been living ever since. We share a small apartment with another Somali woman and her daughter.

It is Ramadan once more, and I am fasting, because it is one of the five pillars of Islam. We human beings have made many mistakes and this is when we can ask forgiveness. During this month, the night becomes alive. When I think of Mogadishu, it is the night that I remember. But I cannot see the moon from here. Sometimes I hardly see the sky for days because of the clouds and fog. Yesterday it was clear, and when I looked up I could almost convince myself that I was seeing the night sky from my old home. I wondered if my husband and daughters were looking at those same stars as they passed over Somalia. On one night during the month of Ramadan called Al-Qadr *they say that Allah will grant the prayers which come from your heart.*

When I think about my family in Somalia, I remember that the children, even during the war, had moments when they laughed and played with each other, unaware of what was going on around them. Their happiness is what I remember most. And when I think of my husband, I always picture him before the war, in the days when we were planning our wedding, before his position became so difficult.

It was during this same holy month of Ramadan that the Dutch authorities told me that we would have to leave the Asylum Seekers' Center. I said I had nowhere else to go. I don't have a passport, or a ticket. I have no money. I can't speak the language. I have never even been out on to the streets of the town. But they kept telling me we would have to go. They came to the door at all hours of the day and night. They even said that the police were going to evict us from the house. I could not believe they would force me out on to the streets with my five-year-old son. But I had no one to go to. There was no one to help us. One night I was cooking the evening meal and we were preparing to break our fast when they came again. I just could not eat, I was so worried and afraid. Ramadan is the most sacred time for a Muslim. But I can't understand how it can be like this. I spend my nights not sleeping because I don't know what I shall do if they force us out of this place and into the streets.

Seynab Azir Wardeere, Asylum Seekers' Center,
Osdorp, The Netherlands, December 2000

In truth, We have sent this Koran down in the night of *Al-Qadr.*
Worshipping Allah on that night is better
than worshipping Him for a thousand months,
because it is then that the angels descend,
by Allah's Permission, with all Decrees.
Throughout that night there is Peace until dawn appears.
Then Allah will make his decrees on matters of death, birth,
provision, and calamities for the coming year.

(97)

It is a blessed night when the angels and inspirations
come down on this earth.
The night of nobility in which believers have
the chance of experiencing perfect happiness.
It is always a clear night with the sacred moments
attended by a cool breeze and gentle rain
which gives excitement and pleasure to the soul.
Those pious people, deep in devotion and prayer,
find a strange happiness
and satisfaction in it—a spiritual experience.

On this night prayers from the heart are met.

(Hadîth)

The United Nations Convention on the Rights of the Child, September 2, 1990

Article 22

Parties shall take appropriate measures to ensure that a child who is seeking refugee status or who is considered a refugee in accordance with applicable international or domestic law and procedures shall, whether unaccompanied or accompanied by his or her parents or by any other person, receive appropriate protection and humanitarian assistance in the enjoyment of applicable rights set forth in the present Convention and in other international human rights or humanitarian instruments to which the said States are Parties

1990 The first group of ten Somalis arrived in The Netherlands in 1984 after fleeing the repression of the Siad Barre regime. By the end of 1990 there are 4,776 Somalis living in The Netherlands.

1991 After sporadic fighting from 1988 onward, civil war breaks out in Somalia.
May 15 A group of 34 Somalis, including Faduma Megag Samater and her four children, arrive at Schiphol airport. Samater's husband, Yussuf Ibrahim Gedi, who has been a resident with refugee status for two and a half years, is waiting for the family at the airport. Despite their request for asylum, Faduma and her children are refused entry. The group is sent back by plane to Rome and then to Ethiopia, a country also in a state of unrest. Despite attempts to trace them, all the Somalis in the group have disappeared.

During fierce fighting in Mogadishu, Seynab Azir Wardeere flees her home and gives birth to her first child, Fatuma, in the mosque that she has visited since childhood.

1992 *Seynab gives birth to her second child, Aisha, at home.*

1993 By this time 15,062 Somalis are living in The Netherlands.

1994 January 1 The Dutch Ministry of Justice cancels the rights of high appeal for all asylum seekers. In previous years the Somalis were eligible for A (political) or C (humanitarian) status which allowed them to stay in The Netherlands.
This is now replaced by a temporary permit to stay which can be revoked at any moment. The Dutch government accepts the proposal but the Justices object, establishing the *Rechtseenheidkamer* (REK), the highest court for Asylum and Migration Law.

1995 A Dutch Ministry of Foreign Affairs report declares that repatriation is possible to parts of northern Somalia. In the course of the year the Ministry of Justice and officials from the Dutch Embassy in Nairobi visit Somalia and establish "agreements" for the return of refused asylum seekers.
June 23 The State Secretary of Justice writes to Parliament declaring an end to the tolerant policy toward Somalis. Temporary permits will be revoked and repatriation resumed.

November 7 The United Nations High Commission for Refugees (UNHCR) in The Hague accepts the new policy but warns that there is a lack of central authority in Somalia and that the human rights situation is precarious.
November 10 Amnesty International Amsterdam expresses to the State Secretary of Justice its concern over refugees who return to Somalia. There is no security or functioning infrastructure in most urban areas and much of Somalia has been destroyed by years of war.
December 8 The courts in Zwolle and The Hague confirm the new policy.

Seynab's family flee their home in Mogadishu and hide in the bush, building a makeshift shelter from sticks and plastic sheeting. Here, Seynab gives birth to her first son, Mohammed.

1996 February 23 The State Secretary of Justice writes to Parliament to explain the repatriation policy. At this time 23,763 Somalis are living in The Netherlands.
March 19 The government of Somaliland (which declared its independence from Somalia in 1991 but which remains internationally unrecognized) states that it will accept voluntary Somali returnees in return for aid to rebuild the country. Returnees must have local confirmation that they have family to receive them. If not, their application will be rejected.
May 23 The Dutch Ministry of Justice plans for between 20 and 40 Somalis to be deported on June 15. The Netherlands is the first European country to establish "agreements" with local leaders in Somalia.
June Dutch officials call UNHCR in Djibouti requesting cooperation in the return of the refugees from The Netherlands. UNHCR refuses.

June 12 The Dutch Immigration and Naturalization Service (IND) orders the deportation of four Somalis taken from their homes in the early morning and brought to the airport by immigration officials. They are not voluntary returnees. They are accompanied by officials on a KLM flight to Nairobi where Dutch IND officials arrange to fly them to southwest Somalia. Before departure, the Dutch Embassy in Nairobi warns the Dutch government that the situation in southern Somalia remains volatile. On arrival in Garbahare the plane is fired on by local militia and the Dutch officials and pilot are held hostage for several days. A ransom is demanded. Non-governmental organization leaders who have established relationships with the local elders ask them to intercede and the Dutch are allowed to leave. The four Somalis, three men and one woman, are released. Months later two of them are traced to Nairobi; the woman has never been found.
June 16 The Dutch Authority charters a Martinair flight for the forced deportation of 19 Somalis to Somaliland. The Djibouti government refuses landing rights and the flight is canceled. Instead, nine security escorts and one IND official accompany the group on a KLM flight to Dubai. The official carries $40,000 for payment of "fees" and a charter flight from Dubai to Somaliland. In Dubai, the Somalis refuse to disembark. The airport officials object to the use of force in "handling" passengers. The IND official argues that the Somalis could be removed but acknowledges the risk of harming members of the group which includes women and children. Finally the plane leaves for Dhaka where it is hoped that transport can be arranged for the group to Hargeisa, the capital of Somaliland. When this proves impossible, the plane returns to Dubai. Once again the group refuses to leave the plane. More than 24 hours later, the plane returns to Schiphol airport. The men are transferred to Tilburg prison where they are kept for one month for failing to cooperate with the Dutch authorities. The women are taken to the detention center at

Ter Apel. Later reports confirm that one of the men suffered psychological trauma following the incident. After their release, most of the group flee the country or disappear.
June 19 The government of Somaliland issues a letter warning all airlines and shipping agencies not to "dump" Somalis in their country.
July The Dutch Parliament continues to support the policy of the Minister of Justice toward repatriation.
August A forced deportation attempt is thwarted by grassroots Dutch and Somali activists in The Netherlands. The IND and Parliament halt the forced deportations to await the decision of the court in Zwolle.
September 3 The court in Zwolle decides that deportation is allowed only if the extended family is known and able to receive the returnee.
October The State Secretary for Justice declares her intention to consult the UNHCR about conditions for safe return. She puts the case before the REK.

1997 The Ministry of Foreign Affairs declares that Somalis may be deported to areas of the country which are safe, in particular northern Somalia and Somaliland. Somalis from the South with clan members in the North may be told to repatriate to the North, despite never having lived there and having no relatives in the region. In the deportation policy, clan background prevails over last residence.
March 6 The REK decides that Somalis coming from northern Somalia or having a clear clan relation there can be sent back.
March 12 Parliament approves the deportation of between 2,000 and 3,000 Somalis to northern Somalia. The State Secretary of Justice requests them to return voluntarily, but if they refuse, they will be forcibly returned.
March 26 President Egal of Somaliland writes to the State Secretary of Justice in The Netherlands: "I hope you can understand the pain and the futility of exchanging the designation of refugee for that of a displaced person in a country that has just emerged from a period of anarchy and chaos, which is still full of landmines and which is totally ignored and ostracized by the international community and cannot make ends meet. I cannot condone or authorize the return of people to whom I can give neither protection nor the necessities of life."
June 24 The government of Somaliland enters into negotiations with the Ministry of Justice and International Organization for Migration (IOM) for the return of refused asylum seekers. The "agreement," which remains informal, will come into force in 1998.
July 5 The Dutch newspaper *Trouw* reports: "Ministry bought false passports for Somalis." A translator for the Ministry of Justice explains that the Ministry gave him the order to buy fake passports for rejected asylum seekers who want to return to their country of origin "voluntarily." According to the Ministry, the fact that no country recognizes the papers does not matter as the people can return to Somalia with them.
July 23 A fact-finding mission from Somaliland visits The Netherlands and after meeting the Somali community rejects the June "agreement" after it is clear that no concrete aid will be given for the rehabilitation of their region.
September 8 The State Secretary of Justice writes to Parliament stating that "the person who does not want to use the IOM program in cooperation with his return, will be put out of the facilities [housing, welfare, health care]."

1998 January 19–21 The Tri-Partite Agreement is signed in Hargeisa between the Somaliland government and the IOM and IND. This provides for the return of voluntary returnees and refused asylum seekers. Somaliland will issue documents for passage. These documents are internationally

unrecognized but without travel papers the IOM cannot make provision for the return.
May 7 The State Secretary of Justice informs Parliament that she has given the IND the order to begin the repatriation.
May 30 The IOM confirms it can facilitate passage only if the applicant has valid travel documents.
September The IOM in The Hague declares that travel documents and tickets are still awaiting negotiations.
October The press reports that the return project for refused asylum seekers is a disaster.
November Amnesty International declares that areas deemed safe by the Dutch government are not always safe. The Dutch Refugee Council declares the return policy unreliable.
December A change in Dutch law now requires any person from any other country wishing to join their spouse, or who is marrying a Dutch citizen, to apply in their home country for Dutch residence. Those Somalis living in The Netherlands without status must go back to Somalia to apply for residency. If the person has children, the children must also leave the country. As there is no Dutch Embassy in Somalia, Somalis wishing to marry or who have been denied status must go to the Dutch Embassy in the nearest country (either Ethiopia or Kenya) to seek resident status.
December Somaliland informs the IOM that the project will be temporarily suspended.

1999 January 23 Somaliland declares to the Ministry of Justice a temporary suspension of the returnees project.
February 3 It is reported in the *Trouw* that the Ministry of Justice is not impressed with the Somaliland resolution and says that they do not need the return agreement to deport refused asylum seekers. Somaliland passports are not recognized internationally.
September 5 Somaliland informs the Ministry of Justice that the Tri-Partite Agreement is officially over.
October 19 The United Nations declares that there is no representative to the Somali mission to the UN and that, although a seat at the UN remains, there is no official who can issue travel documents.

In Mogadishu, four armed men enter Seynab's family home. They kill her father and attack her. Her three children are present. A week later Seynab's mother dies. Their home is traded for passage to Europe, but there is only sufficient money for two people to travel. The family separates. Seynab and her son Mohammed leave the country. Seynab's husband and two daughters travel to his family in Baidoa.

2000 August Warmoog Amir Hussein and her 18-month-old baby are evicted from the Asylum Seekers' Center (AZC) in Osdorp. Warmoog arrived in The Netherlands in April 1999. Her son Mahan was born in The Netherlands and received the standard first refusal for refugee status from the Dutch authorities. Warmoog's court-appointed attorney neglected to file an appeal in time. Her case was closed with a negative judgment and she and her son were put out on to the streets. Although grassroots Dutch attorneys launched an appeal and the court declared that she had a good case because she came from a vulnerable group, she was denied access to housing by the Central Organization for Housing and Asylum Seekers (COA).

December 1 *Friday, a Muslim holy day during the holy month of Ramadan. Seynab and her five-year-old son Mohammed are ordered out of the AZC at Osdorp. Mohammed is barred from the school he has been attending since arrival in The*

Netherlands. No provision is made for a passport, ticket, money, food, or an alternative place to live.

December 8 Yusuf Salah and his wife Luul Mohammed Abdi Rahman arrived in The Netherlands as asylum seekers in 1995. They have lived in the country without status for nearly six years, during which time their four children were born. Without warning, the family are evicted from the AZC and begin life on the streets.

2001 January The former Prime Minister of The Netherlands, Ruud Lubbers, is appointed United Nations High Commissioner for Refugees.
March 15 At the final meeting of the REK, the Dutch policy toward asylum seekers is challenged by the Lawyers' Association of the Center City. Under the current law an asylum seeker may ask for asylum for the second time. However, the act of filing such a request means that the asylum seeker must immediately leave the shelter and go through the procedure from the street. If no request is made they may remain in the shelter until such time as they are expelled. If the asylum seeker is fortunate, they may be in the AZCs for years before action is taken on their case.
March 15 A Somali woman who arrived in The Netherlands in 1995 and subsequently married a Dutch naturalized Somali, and whose three children were born in The Netherlands, is refused residency. She and her children are told to go back to Somalia where they may apply for resident status in The Netherlands. The Lawyers' Association of the Center City pleads for leniency, citing Article 8 of the European Charter against sending children or their caretaker back into a warring environment. The lawyer for the Ministry of Justice argues that Article 8 is not a defense because the woman elected to bear children while her status was undecided. The Lawyers' Association of the Center City points out that there is no body which can issue official travel documents to Somalis. The attorney for the Ministry of Justice states that: "if a country will accept the backside of a cigarette package for a document, then it doesn't matter what they use when returning as long as they go." The Lawyers' Association of the Center City confirms that the Ministry of Justice attorney is, in effect, asking Somalis to obtain false documents.
March 27 The Lawyers' Association of the Center City requests a court investigation as to whether the State Secretary of Justice is encouraging Somalis to obtain false documents. This would constitute complicity in forgery and fraud under section 231 of the Dutch penal code and if proven would carry a four-year prison sentence.
March 27 Somali and Dutch grassroots organizations and individuals submit a petition with 2,000 names to the Parliament requesting that Somalis who applied for asylum prior to April 1998 and who have remained in limbo for more than three years be given full resident status and permission to stay in The Netherlands.
March 27 An Amsterdam court rules in the case of Warmoog Amir Hussein, confirming that the law which allowed her to be evicted from the AZC (Stappenplan 2000, RVA 1997) is technically flawed and therefore invalid. Another case pending at the Hogeraad Court concerns the rights to sustenance of several thousand Somalis and many more asylum seekers. If the prior ruling is overthrown, these people will keep the right to remain in the AZCs without being evicted. For the unknown number of people already put out into the streets during the years in which the law was in effect there is no recourse to action.

April 2001

- The new Aliens Act takes effect limiting the asylum seeking process and confining the rights of appeal.
- The Council of State (Raad van State) takes over from the more liberal REK in Asylum and Migration Law. The Council of State is not obliged to give the grounds for its decisions.
- The Ministry of the Interior puts the current Somali population in The Netherlands at 30,000. This figure does not represent those persons under the age of 12, therefore the actual number is significantly higher.
- Many Somalis have remained in the AZCs for up to seven years without any decision being made as to their status. They live with the imminent threat of deportation. Hundreds of Somalis have been evicted, or are in the process of being evicted from AZCs. Some of them will be expelled before they can avail themselves of due process.
- Somalia has no central authority and no country maintains diplomatic relationships with it.
- Half of the world's refugees are children.
- The UN lists Somalia as the poorest country on earth.

European Convention on Human Rights

Article 3

No one shall be subjected to torture or to inhuman or degrading treatment or punishment.

Article 8

Everyone has the right to respect for his private and family life, his home and his correspondence. There shall be no interference by a public authority with the exercise of this right except such as is in accordance with the law and is necessary in a democratic society in the interests of national security, public safety or the economic well-being of the country, for the prevention of disorder or crime, for the protection of health or morals, or for the protection of the rights and freedoms of others.

At the time of this book's printing, a ruling on an emergency appeal of Seynab Azir Wardeere's case is pending. A Somali lawyer practicing in The Netherlands, Musse Hersi, who heard of her case, brought it to Vincent Kuit at the Lawyers' Association of the Center City. The emergency appeal was launched challenging the technical basis of the eviction order in an effort to thwart the physical expulsion notice. Had it not been for this, Seynab and her son would already be living on the streets without shelter. A further appeal based on her medical evidence has been submitted along with a request for asylum on humanitarian grounds. The lawyer for the State has postponed the case repeatedly. The Central Organization for Housing and Asylum Seekers continues to insist that Seynab be removed from the Asylum Seekers' Center at Osdorp. Mohammed remains with his mother. Seynab has had no word on the whereabouts of her husband and two daughters.

Ramadan Moon is the second in a series of projects intended to further awareness of international human rights issues

Copies of *Ramadan Moon* and its companion volume, *A Camel for the Son*, the first project in the series, are being distributed throughout The Netherlands to parliamentarians, judges, mayors, and the media, in a collaborative effort with both Dutch and Somali organizations to create a policy more sympathetic to all asylum seekers who flee their countries in pursuit of safety

Generous support for the first two projects in the human rights series has been provided by the Volkart Foundation, Winterthur, Switzerland

The *Ramadan Moon* traveling exhibition, at the Nederlands Foto Instituut, Rotterdam, from March 17 to May 6, 2001, is supported by a grant from Photowork(s) in Progress, an initiative of the Nederlands Foto Instituut and the Mondriaan Foundation

For more information on this project and *A Camel for the Son*, or to order a book, visit www.fazalsheikh.org

Religious texts drawn from the Qur'an, King Fahd Complex for the printing of the Holy Qur'an, Madinah, KSA cite the *Sûrah* followed by the *Ayât* number. The *Hadîth* are drawn from the volumes of the *Sahih Al-Bukhâri.*

Fazal Sheikh—Ramadan Moon
Editing: Liz Jobey, London
Design: Fazal Sheikh / Hanna Koller, Zurich
Translation: Hassan M. Khalief, English–Somali; Karen de Wit, English–Dutch, Holland
Historical advisors: Musse A. Hersi, Vincent Kuit, Riemke Rip, Annemieke de Wit, Holland
Separations: Steidl, K. Töpfer, Göttingen, Germany
Production: Steidl, Göttingen

First edition 2001 ISBN 0-9707613-1-7
Printed in Germany

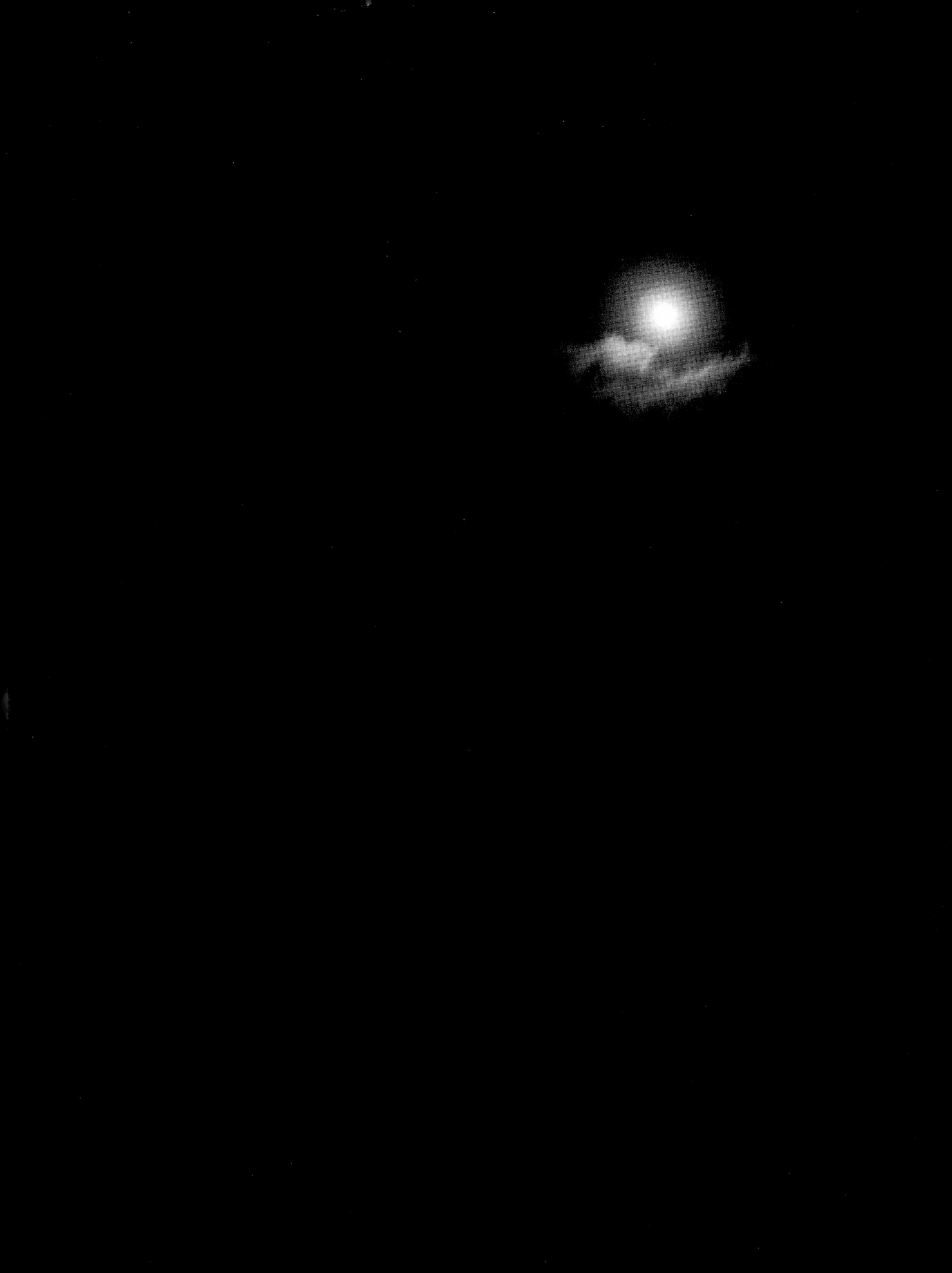

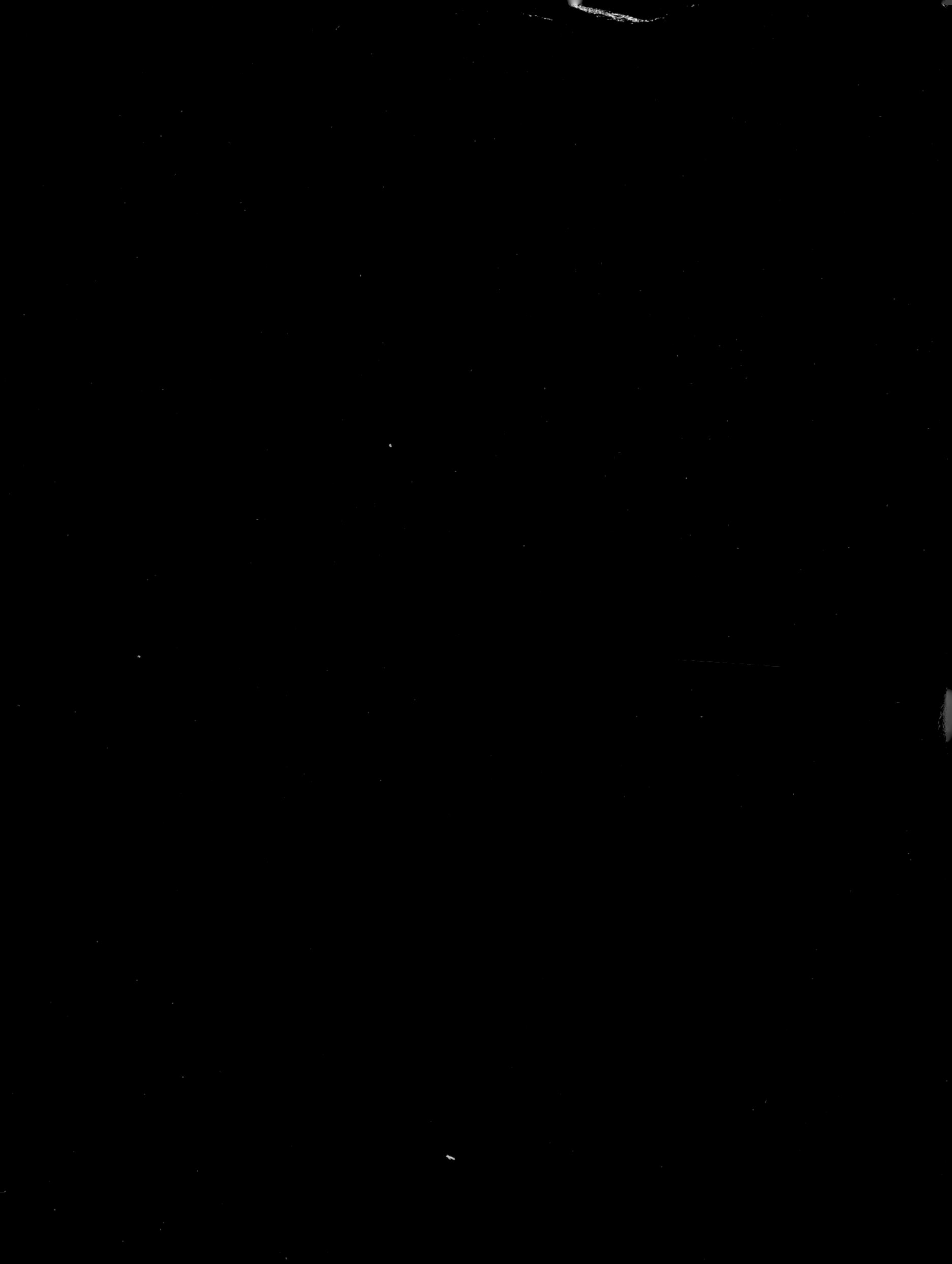